BOSTON

A PHOTOGRAPHIC PORTRAIT

First published in the United States of America by
Twin Lights Publishers, Inc.
10 Hale Street
Rockport, Massachusetts 01966
Telephone: (978) 546-7398
http://www.twinlightspub.com

ISBN 1-885435-21-5

10 9 8 7 6 5 4 3 2 1

Book design by
SYP Design & Production
http://www.sypdesign.com

Front Cover Photo by: Len Wickens
Back Cover Photos by: Andrew P. Douglas,
Joan R. Dunne, Sarah Lannon and Babs Amour

Printed in China

Other titles in the Photographic Portrait series:

Cape Ann
Kittery to the Kennebunks
The Mystic Coast, Stonington to New London
The White Mountains
Boston's South Shore
Upper Cape Cod
The Rhode Island Coast
Greater Newburyport
Portsmouth and Coastal New Hampshire
Naples, Florida
Sarasota, Florida
The British Virgin Islands
Portland, Maine
Mid and Lower Cape Cod
The Berkshires
Camden, Maine
The Champlain Valley

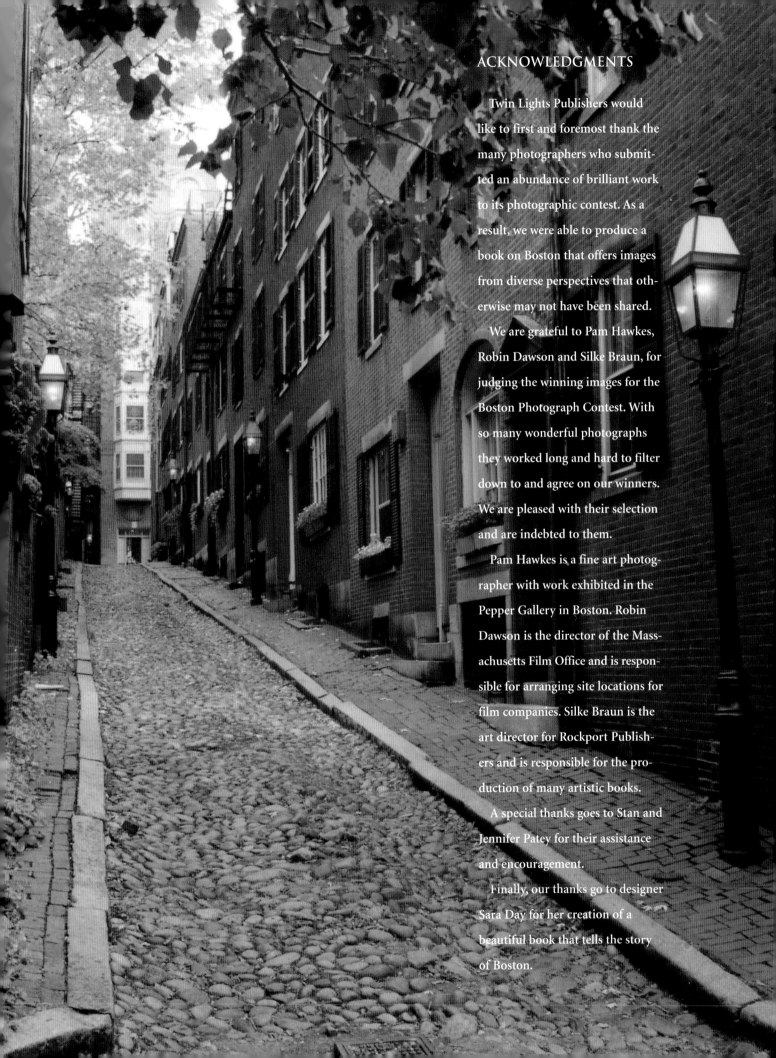

ACKNOWLEDGMENTS

Twin Lights Publishers would like to first and foremost thank the many photographers who submitted an abundance of brilliant work to its photographic contest. As a result, we were able to produce a book on Boston that offers images from diverse perspectives that otherwise may not have been shared.

We are grateful to Pam Hawkes, Robin Dawson and Silke Braun, for judging the winning images for the Boston Photograph Contest. With so many wonderful photographs they worked long and hard to filter down to and agree on our winners. We are pleased with their selection and are indebted to them.

Pam Hawkes is a fine art photographer with work exhibited in the Pepper Gallery in Boston. Robin Dawson is the director of the Massachusetts Film Office and is responsible for arranging site locations for film companies. Silke Braun is the art director for Rockport Publishers and is responsible for the production of many artistic books.

A special thanks goes to Stan and Jennifer Patey for their assistance and encouragement.

Finally, our thanks go to designer Sara Day for her creation of a beautiful book that tells the story of Boston.

second place

RAILROAD BRIDGE

KEVIN AND SUSAN PSAROS
NIKON N90S, FUJI VELVIA

Early morning light casts a
perfect reflection of this South
Boston Bridge.

The Psaros' picture of the Old Colony Bridge in South Boston was taken early one morning while Kevin was on his way to work. He remembers it as a sight he had wanted to photograph many times but hadn't until this particular day. the Psaros' passion lies primarily with nature and wildlife photography. They've established a Fine Art and Stock Photography business and have exhibited their work in many local venues as well as been published both locally and nationally. Their website address is www.natureartists.com/psarosks.htm.

third place

CHURCH AND HANCOCK TOWER

RICHARD FERRARA
MINOLTA X370N, KODAK EKTAR125, F/5.6

The Romanesque style of architect Henry Richardson is revealed in this glimpse of the Trinity Church reflected in the John Hancock Tower.

Richard Ferrara has been an avid photographer since he was a teenager. In his view, photography is all about finding new perspectives. He likes to experiment with different angles and vantage points, often capturing reflected images and focusing in on detailed pieces of the bigger picture as shown by his winning image. Originally from Cranston, RI, Richard moved to Boston in 1982 where he attended Emerson College. After living in the city for 12 years, he moved to Amesbury, MA in 1995. Richard's e-mail address is sightsee@worldnet.att.net.

THE PARTISANS

WILLIAM MATTERN
CANON REBEL, FUJI 100

The Partisans, located on the Boston Common, is a tribute to freedom fighters everywhere. Polish artist, Andrzei Pitynski, created this sculpture in 1979 and has loaned it to the city for display.

left

FREEDOM TRAIL BEGINS

SARAH LANNON
OLYMPUS ZOOM 140

The freedom trail begins on the Boston Common and ends at Bunker Hill Monument. Follow the red brick trail to the 16 historical sites in Boston.

opposite

GOLDEN DOME

ARLENE F. TALIADOROS
NIKON N90 , FUJI 400

The 24-karat gold leaf dome of the State House catches the sun in every season. Originally made of wood and later covered with copper by Paul Revere, the dome was gilded in 1872. During WWII the dome was painted black to disguise the landmark.

BOSTON PUBLIC GARDEN

RICHARD ADAMS
NIKON N90, FUJI VELVIA, F/11

Public Garden flowers delight the
eye from spring through fall.

MAKE WAY FOR DUCKLINGS

MARCELLA WAGNER
CANON EOS ELAN II, TAMRON 28-300 F/6.7

Mrs. Mallard and her 8 ducklings:
Jack, Kick, Lack, Mack, Knack, Ouack,
Pack and Quack can be seen along a
35 foot cobblestone pathway in the
Boston Public Garden. Inspired by
the children's book by Robert
McCloskey, *Make Way For Ducklings*,
Nancy Schon completed this sculp-
ture in 1987 for the enjoyment of
children throughout the world.

above

54TH REGIMENT MEMORIAL

WILLIAM J. FERRERA
PEN TAX SPOTMATIC, KODACHROME 64

On May 28, 1863 a voluntary regiment of 1000 African-American soldiers, the first black regiment from the north, marched off to fight in the civil war. This monument was unveiled 34 years later on the Boston Common on Memorial Day of 1897. Since then this large bronze sculpture has gained international attention.

opposite

GEORGE WASHINGTON

MARCELLA WAGNER
CANON EOS ELAN II, KODAK E100 VS

George Washington astride his horse Nelson stands watch at the entrance to the Boston Public Garden.

above

BOSTON PUBLIC GARDEN

RICHARD ADAMS
NIKON N90, FUJI VELVIA, F/11

Public Garden flowers delight the eye from spring through fall.

opposite

MAKE WAY FOR DUCKLINGS

MARCELLA WAGNER
CANON EOS ELAN II, TAMRON 28-300 F/6.7

Mrs. Mallard and her 8 ducklings: Jack, Kick, Lack, Mack, Knack, Ouack, Pack and Quack can be seen along a 35 foot cobblestone pathway in the Boston Public Garden. Inspired by the children's book by Robert McCloskey, *Make Way For Ducklings*, Nancy Schon completed this sculpture in 1987 for the enjoyment of children throughout the world.

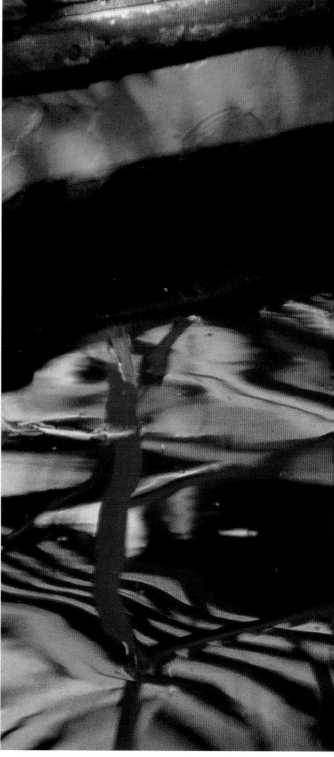

top

FROG POND

RICHARD ADAMS
NIKON N90, FUJI VELVIA, F/16

The swan boats pause for a rest at the end of a busy day.

bottom

SWAN BOATS

GORAN MATIJASEVIC
MINOLTA, KODACHROME 64

Swan boats have been meandering around the lagoon in the Public Garden since 1877 when an English immigrant, Robert Paget, invented them. They have been in the Paget family ever since.

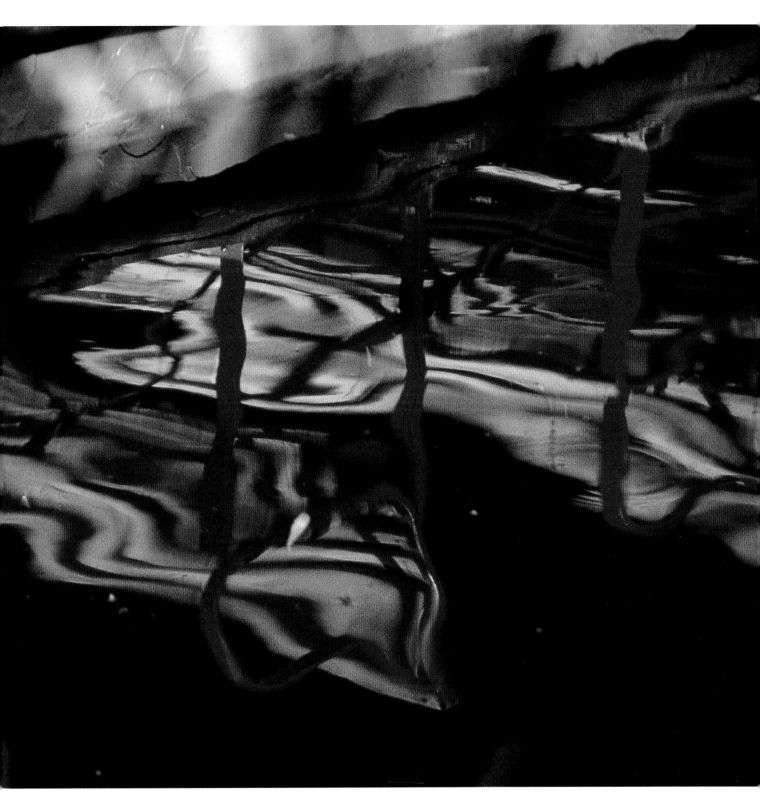

above

REFLECTIONS OF
SWAN BOATS

BABS ARMOUR
NIKON 6006, FUJI VELVIA

The early morning light creates
swan boat reflections in the lagoon
of the Public Garden.

right

TOP OF THE OLD STATE HOUSE

VIVIAN FRINK
CANON AE 1, KODAK KODACHROME

The prominent feature of the Old State House is its tall multi-part steeple with elaborate clear glass windows.

below

BOSTON S FINEST

BARBARA ROSS
LEICA R8, EKTACHROME 200, F/5.6

Boston's finest bundled up to patrol the Boston Common on a winter day.

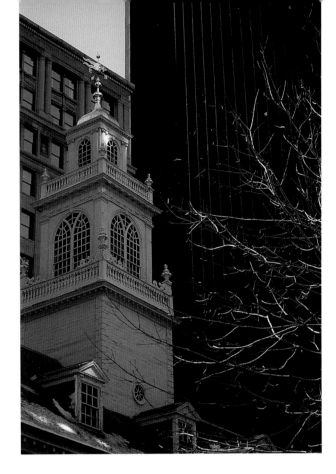

CANADA GOOSE WITH GOSLINGS

KEVIN AND SUSAN PSAROS
NIKON N905 FUJI VELVIA

Well known as a birding destination, Canada Geese find their way to the Mt. Auburn Cemetery and make it their home.

opposite

SPRING IN BLOOM

KEVIN AND SUSAN PSAROS
NIKON N90S, FUJI VELVIA

Mt. Auburn Cemetery, located in Cambridge, is well known for it's landscaping and flowers whose collection dates back to 1831. This experimental garden started by the Massachusetts Horticultural Society was to become the first garden cemetery in this country.

CUSTOM HOUSE

RICHARD ADAMS
NIKON N90, FUJI VELVI, F/8

The Custom House was originally a four-faced Greek temple built of Rockport granite in 1847. The tower, with its 22-foot clock, was added in 1915 and has become a city icon.

above

DEPARTMENT STORE AT DUSK.

GORAN MATIJASEVIC
MINOLTA, FUJICHROME 100

It's nearing closing time for stores
in the city.

left

PARK STREET CHURCH

GORAN MATIJASEVIC
MINOLTA, KODACHROME 64

The Park Street Church, dating back
to 1809, is the site of the old town
granary where grain was kept before
the revolution. The Granary Burying Ground was founded in 1660
and is the third oldest burying
ground in Boston.

opposite

SKY ROCKETS IN FLIGHT

JANE PEDERSEN
OLYMPUS SENSIO 100 FILM

Fireworks light up the sky along the
Charles River on the 4th of July.

right

UNDER THE DOME

MICHAEL LEONARD
CANON TX, FUJI ASTIA 100

A brass floor-marker, located under the dome of Quincy Market, signifies the year this 535 foot long building was completed.

below

QUINCY MARKET

RICHARD ADAMS
NIKON N90, FUJI VELVIA, F/5.6

Quincy Market and The Custom House are aglow for the holidays.

opposite

GRASSHOPPER

MICHAEL LEONARD
CANON TX, FUJI ASTIA 100

The four-foot grasshopper weathervane topping Faneuil Hall has its roots in London. Fashioned after the weathervane atop the London Royal Exchange, a similar one was placed on Faneuil Hall with the hope that Boston would become the financial center of the new world.

SNOW STORM

RICHARD FERRARA
VIVITAR XV1 , KODAK 100, F/5.6

Marlboro Street in the Back Bay
after a snowstorm.

opposite

WINTER ON
MT. VERNON STREET

HELEN EDDY

Mt. Vernon Street is encrusted in
snow on this cold morning on
Beacon Hill.

top

MAKE WAY FOR DUCKLINGS

HELEN EDDY

Topped with winter hats, Mrs. Mallard leads her ducklings through the Boston Public Garden.

bottom

ENTRANCE TO BOSTON PUBLIC GARDEN

HELEN EDDY

Even in the winter, the Boston Public Garden is an inviting park to stroll through.

opposite

JOHN HANCOCK TOWER

HOWARD M. GOODMAN
CANON REBEL 2000, KODAK E100 VS, F/5.6

A clear view of the John Hancock Tower may be seen from the Boston Common.

CUSTOM HOUSE

RICHARD ADAMS
NIKON N90, FUJI VELVI, F/8

The Custom House was originally a four-faced Greek temple built of Rockport granite in 1847. The tower, with its 22-foot clock, was added in 1915 and has become a city icon.

SAMUEL ADAMS

MICHAEL LEONARD
CANON TX , FUJI ASTIA 100

A major leader in the American
Revolution, Samuel Adams often
met at Faneuil Hall to rally the
citizens of Boston to the cause
of independence.

above

MASS STATE HOUSE

VIVIAN FRINK
CANON AE 1, KODAK KODACHROME

The Massachusetts State House is
the oldest building on Beacon Hill,
with its cornerstones laid in 1795
by Samuel Adams and Paul Revere.
Boston architect Charles Bulfinch
adapted the magnificent Greek and
Roman temples for the new State
House. After 3 years of construc-
tion, the new State House was
completed in 1798.

right

ARCHWAYS

LEN WICKENS
RICON, FUJI 100

Archways along the Columbus
Park provide shade for afternoon
strollers.

left

RED

DAVID F. GOUVEIA
NIKON, KODAK, F/3.5

Red Auerbach and his winning cigar
are located at Quincy Market. A
memorable figure among fans, Red
was known for his habit of waiting
to light his cigar until he was cer-
tain that the Celtics would win
their game.

right

BREWER FOUNTAIN

ANDREW P. DOUGLASS
MINOLTA, EPP

Bought as a souvenir at the 1867
Paris Exposition, Mr. Gardner
Brewer donated this fountain to the
city where it rests in the Boston
Common. Made of bronze and
granite, the fountain represents
mythological water deities Neptune,
Amphiltrite, Acis and Galatea.

opposite

OLD CITY HALL

SARAH LANNON
OLYMPUS ZOOM 140

Built in 1865, this building served as
Boston's City Hall until 1969. Today,
retail and office tenants occupy it.
The new city hall is located just one
block away.

BOSTON GARDEN

ANDREW P. DOUGLASS
MILOLTA, GC

Replaced in 1995 by the Fleet
Center, the 1928 Boston Garden
will forever be in the hearts of
true Celtics and Bruins fans. Here,
the Garden is set up and ready for
the Celtics.

above

**SUN RISING, MOON
SETTING**

RODNEY R. HARRIS
CANON ELAN IIE, KODAK
ECKTACHROME 100, F/16

The sun begins to rise while the
moon hangs over Long Wharf.

SUMMER CELEBRATION

JANE PEDERSEN
OLYMPUS SENSIO 100 FILM

Fireworks along the Charles on the 4th of July.

PATH OF PANSIES

KEVIN AND SUSAN PSAROS
NIKON N905, KODAK 100

The 164 acres at the Mt. Auburn
Cemetery blossom with about a
thousand varieties of trees, flowers
and shrubs. Bird clubs meet in the
spring and welcome you to join.

SPRINGTIME IN THE GARDENS

ROBERT A. DENNIS
NIKON N70, KODAK GOLD 200

Red tulips usher in the beginning
of spring in the Boston Public
Garden.

above

QUINCY MARKET

SARAH LANNON

Quincy Market, located directly behind Faneuil Hall, served as the cities wholesale food distribution center for 170 years. Today, visitors can still find culinary delights throughout the market.

opposite, top

QUINCY MARKET AT CHRISTMAS TIME

JOAN R. DUNNE
MINOLTA 5000, KODAK GOLD 400, AUTO

Holiday lights and a horse drawn carriage welcome visitors to Quincy Market.

opposite, bottom

SPRINGTIME IN THE PUBLIC GARDEN

JOAN R. DUNNE
MINOLTA 5000, KODAK GOLD 400, AUTO

A warm spring day attracts visitors to the Public Garden. Blooming Dogwood and Magnolia trees provide a peaceful atmosphere.

top and bottom

QUINCY MARKET

GORAN MATIJASEVIC
WIDELUX, FUJICHROME 100
MINOLTA, KODACHROME 64

Local artisans and entrepreneurs ped-
dle their crafts in small carts along
the perimeter of Quincy Market.

opposite

FANEUIL HALL MARKET

LEN WICKENS
RICON, FUJI 100

Wealthy merchant, Peter Faneuil,
originally built Boston's first marketplace, Faneuil Hall, in 1742. During
the pre-revolutionary period, Faneuil
Hall became a meeting place of
ideas. Today the marketplace offers
visitors a unique array of shops.

Flower Show ⬇ FREE Admission

left

TREMONT STREET

MARCELLA WAGNER
CANON EOS ELAN II , KODAK E100 VS, F/9.5

Christmas décor on Tremont Street,
along the Public Garden.

below

BULL & FINCH

MARCELLA WAGNER
CANON EOS ELAN II , KODAK E100 VS, F/9.5

The Bull & Finch Pub on Beacon Street
was established in 1968 and was the
inspiration for the hit TV series, *Cheers*
where "everybody knows your name."

DAWN SKY

PETER RICHMAN
NIKON N80, FUJI REOLA

Early morning lights surrounding the
Public Garden illuminate the lagoon.
The day is just unfolding.

right

YESTERYEARS

VIVIAN FRINK
CANON AE 1, KODAK KODACHROME

Lavender tinted glass along Beacon Street.

below

LOUISBURG SQUARE

HOWARD M. GOODMAN
CANON REBEL 2000, KODAK E100 VS, F/5.6

On the west side of Louisburg Square, Beacon Hill, an American flag is flown with pride.

opposite

CLASSIC ENTRANCE

ARLENE F. TALIADOROS
NIKON N90, FUJI 400

Residences on Beacon Hill are accented with tastefully decorative doorways.

above and left

SOUTH END ENTRANCES

JOAN R. DUNNE
MINOLTA 5000, KODAK GOLD 400, AUTO

Row houses with bow fronts are
adorned with flowers and foliage.

opposite

BEACON HILL ARCH

LAURA M. DEPAMPHILIS
MINOLTA SRT-SCII, KODAK EKTACHROME

Entranceways catch your eye all along
Beacon Hill.

above

ACORN STREET

HELEN EDDY

Acorn Street, located on Beacon Hill, takes you back in time when life in Boston was quite different than it is now.

opposite

THE BELL IN HAND TAVERN

ANN L. HURD
CANON REBEL 2000, KODAK GOLD 200

Built in 1795, the Bell In Hand Tavern on Union Street continues to serve spirits to its patrons.

ACORN STREET

HELEN EDDY

Acorn Street, located on Beacon Hill, takes you back in time when life in Boston was quite different than it is now.

THE BELL IN HAND TAVERN

ANN L. HURD
CANON REBEL 2000, KODAK GOLD 200

Built in 1795, the Bell In Hand Tavern on Union Street continues to serve spirits to its patrons.

THE GREEN DRAGON TAVERN

ANN L. HURD
CANON REBEL 2000, KODAK GOLD 200

The Green Dragon, near Faneuil Hall on Marshall Street, announces its fare for passersby.

MAMMA MARIA

ANN L. HURD
CANON REBEL 2000, KODAK GOLD 200

Old-style gas lamps adorn the entrance to Mamma Maria's on North Street.

above

CITY LIGHTS

DANIEL RUDHARDT
CANON EOS 500, KODAK ROYAL GOLD 100

The Old State house can be seen in the distance as a cars headlights makes its way through the city.

left

DWARFED BY TIME

BEVERLY GRADY
FUJICA AX3, KODACHROME 64

The Old State House, site of the Boston Massacre, was built in 1713. Today, dwarfed by surrounding buildings, one forgets that this was also the site where citizens gathered on July 18, 1776 to hear the Declaration of Independence read from the second floor balcony.

opposite

CUSTOM HOUSE TOWER AND NORTH

NELSON ROSS
MAMIYA 7, FUJI VELVIA F/5.6

The Custom House, built at the end of the City's docks in 1915, was Boston's first skyscraper. This aerial, taken from the 43rd floor of One International Place, shows how much downtown land was created by landfill.

top

HEAD OF THE CHARLES

WILLIAM MATTERN
CANON REBEL, FUJI 100

The "Head of the Charles" regatta has been taking place every October since 1965. This three-mile race attracts upwards of 250,000 spectators on a beautiful fall day such as this.

bottom

BACK BAY AT SUNRISE

HELEN EDDY

A new day is about to begin in Boston.

COLONEL WILLIAM PRESCOTT

SARAH LANNON
OLYMPUS ZOOM 140

"Don't shoot until you see the whites of their eyes." This famous quote was attributed to Colonel William Prescott who led the colonial forces to Breed's Hill, June 17, 1775. The Bunker Hill Monument was erected in 1842 to commemorate the first major battle of the American Revolution.

HOLOCAUST MEMORIAL

WILLIAM MATTERN
CANON REBEL , FUJI 100

Across from City Hall, the six glass towers that make up the memorial are each etched with one million numbers, symbolizing the six million Jews that perished under the Nazi's. Architect Stanley Saitowitz received the prominent Henry Becan Medal upon its completion in 1995.

above

BIG DIG DINNER

JUDITH AUSTIN BROWN
PENTAX PZ

The Big Dig Diner on Dry Dock Avenue is a culinary training facility for inner city youths. The diner offers a Friday lunch buffet where you can get a turkey dinner with all the fixings for just six dollars.

following page

ROWES WHARF

NELSON ROSS
MAMIYA 7, FUJI VELVIA

This view of Rowes Wharf taken from the new Federal Court House reminds us of Boston's seafaring history.

top

LANDING

MICHAEL LEONARD
CANON TX, FUJI PROVIA 100F, F/5.6,
6 MINUTES 80A FILTER

Airplanes circle over the City
preparing to land at Logan.

bottom

JET TRAIL

ANDREW P. DOUGLASS
MINOLTA, EPP

A jet trail creates a path across the
City's skyline.

opposite

MOORED BOATS

ANDREW P. DOUGLASS
MINOLTA, EPP

The city lights are a breathtaking
backdrop for these boats moored
along the Charles River.

CHINATOWN

LIZ LIGON
CANON, FUJI VELVIA, F11

Firecrackers at the Lion Dance
Festival mark the beginning of the
Chinese New Year.

ROWERS AT SUNRISE

KEVIN AND SUSAN PSAROS
NIKON, FUJI VELVIA, F/100

Rowers view a beautiful sunrise
along the Charles River.

HAY MARKET

WILLIAM J. FERRERA
PENTAX SPOTMATIC, KODACHROME 64

Located in the North End, patrons
buy their fruits, vegetables, and
meats along this outdoor market.

NORTH END MARKET

ANDREW P. DOUGLASS
MINOLTA, EPP

Fruit is abundant along Haymarket
Square.

top

LOWELL HOUSE

DANIEL RUDHARDT
CANON EOS 500, KODAK ROYAL GOLD 100

The moon appears to adorn the top of the Lowell House, at Harvard University. Built in 1930, the Lowell House is one of 13 undergraduate houses at Harvard University.

bottom

COMMUTER DOCK AT ROWES WHARF

SARA B. EDWARDS
NIKON N70, KODAK GOLD 400, F/16

Early morning commuters delight in the breathtaking sunrise off Rowes Wharf.

opposite

TALL SHIP

RICHARD FERRARA
MINOLTA X370N, FUJI 200, F/16

A tall ship is docked near the Charlestown Navy Yard, next to "Old Ironsides."

above

HARBORFEST

RICHARD ADAMS
NIKON N90, FUJI VELVIA, F/11

Boston celebrates its independence
with Harborfest every 4th of July.

opposite, top

TWILIGHT

KEVIN AND SUSAN PSAROS
NIKON N905, KODAK 100

Boston is lit up with a lavender sky
at twilight.

opposite, bottom

BLUE MOON

MICHAEL LEONARD
CANON TX, FUJI PROVIA 100F, F/2.8 10 SEC.

A full moon glows through the
clouds over Boston.

MEMORIAL DRIVE

KEVIN AND SUSAN PSAROS
NIKON, FUJI VELVIA, F/100

Trees line Memorial Drive in Cambridge.

FLOWER SHOW

CYNTHIA R CRONIG
MINOLTA 400SI , KODAK, F/8

The Flower Show, an annual event at the Bayside Exposition, attracts viewers from all over New England.

ROWING ON THE CHARLES

KEVIN AND SUSAN PSAROS
NIKON, FUJI VELVIA, F/100

The Harvard Boat House is the
perfect backdrop for these rowers.

SOUTH SHORE SUNSET

WILLIAM MATTERN
NICROMAT, KODACHROME, F/1.4

Boston's skyline is distinctive over
the water from nearly 20 miles.

right

BARKING CRAB RESTAURANT

BARBARA ROSS
LEICA R8, VELVIA F/4

In the land of bean and cod, the Barking Crab restaurant serves up local color on the wharf on Sleeper Street by Atlantic Avenue.

below

SAILBOAT AT DUSK

KEVIN AND SUSAN PSAROS
NIKON N905, KODAK 100

A colorful sail lights up the harbor at dusk.

opposite

KENNEDY LIBRARY AT COLUMBIA POINT

BARBARA ROSS
LEICA R8, VELVIA F/16

The John Fitzpatrick Kennedy Library was dedicated on October 20, 1979 in memory of our 35th President.

above

KENNEDY LIBRARY AT COLUMBIA POINT

BARBARA ROSS
LEICA R8, VELVIA F/16

Visitors to the Kennedy Library at Columbia Point feel the late president's connection to Boston, across the bay, and to the water.

PIERS PARK

KEVIN AND SUSAN PSAROS
NIKON, KODAK 100, F/100
NIKON, FUJI VELVIA, F/100 (*below*)
NIKON, FUJI VELVIA, F/100 (*opposite*)

In 1995, Massport completed the
spectacular Piers Park in East
Boston. A model sailing center was
designed as a recreational resource
for people of all ages to enjoy.

above

FALL REGATTA

PETER RICHMAN
NIKON N80, FUJI REOLA

This aerial view of the Charles River is the site of the world's largest two-day rowing event. More than 5,400 athletes compete in the "Head of the Charles" regatta.

opposite

WALKERS ON MEMORIAL DRIVE

PETER RICHMAN
NIKON N80, FUJI REOLA

Walkers and joggers take advantage of the fact that Memorial Drive is closed to vehicular traffic on Sundays throughout the spring, summer and fall.

above

BOSTON LIGHT

SAMUEL F MICELI
CANON EOS REBEL, KODAK GOLD 200,
125/F11

Boston Light, originally built on Beacon Island in 1716, was North America's first lighthouse.

left

NANTUCKET II

WILLIAM MATTERN
CANON REBEL, FUJI 100, AUTO

The Nantucket II, built in 1952, is one of 170 lightships that served mariners around the United States. Today, there are just 15 remaining, none of which are in active service. Lightships were assigned the most difficult locations where it was impossible to build a lighthouse.

right

BOAT'S-EYE VIEW

STANLEY A. CRONIG
MAMIYA SEKOR, KODAK, F/11

Boston as seen from the harbor on a clear day.

below

EARLY MORNING

BARBARA ROSS
LEICA R8, VELVIA F/5.6

A tugboat begins its busy schedule as the city dawns a new day.

SAILBOATS ON THE CHARLES

KEVIN AND SUSAN PSAROS
NIKON, KODAK 100, F/100

Sailboats are ready for a day on the
Charles River.

opposite

ENDORPHINE

KEVIN AND SUSAN PSAROS
NIKON, FUJI VELVIA, F/100

Morning light brightens the city skyline
and creates string-like reflections in the
water.

left

CITGO

DOUGLAS MICHAEL HOUSEMAN
NIKON N90S, KODAK EKTACHROME 100
ELITE, F/4

This famous landmark has been lighting up the city since 1965. The first Citgo sign to be placed at this locations was in 1940. It has been replaced several times, but this blue and red version is the one that most Fenway fans identify with.

below

MASS TURNPIKE

DOUGLAS MICHAEL HOUSEMAN
NIKON N90S, KODAK EKTACHROME 100
ELITE, F/8

The Boylston Street bridge offers a night view of the Mass Turnpike. The Turnpike runs 135 miles, from West Stockbridge to 93 in Boston.

above

BOSTON SKYLINE

RICHARD ADAMS
NIKON N90, FUJI VELVI, F/5.6

Boston's skyline is reflected in the
Charles River from Memorial Drive.

right

WANING SUNSET

DOUGLAS MICHAEL HOUSEMAN
NIKON N90S, KODAK EKTACHROME 100
ELITE, F/18

As the sun fades away quietness
descends on Coolidge Corner.

above

FENWAY PARK

GORAN MATIJASEVIC
MINOLTA, FUJICHROME 100

The Prudential offers a grand view of Fenway Park. The Red Sox opened the park in 1912 and fans continue to crowd into its cozy confines decades later.

right

MIDDAY ON COMMONWEALTH AVE

DOUGLAS MICHAEL HOUSMAN
NIKON F5, KODACHROME 64, F/22

The Green Line makes its way up Commonwealth Avenue on a busy afternoon.

opposite

RED SOX TICKET OFFICE

JUDITH AUSTIN BROWN
PENTAX PZ

A familiar sight for Red Sox fans is the ticket office just off Yawkey Way. It appears to be a quiet day with no lines.

FENWAY PARK

GORAN MATIJASEVIC
WIDELUX, FUJICHROME 100

Fenway Park with its bright red bleachers stands out from this view from the Prudential Center. To the left is Northeastern University and The Christian Science Church. To the right are Brookline, the famous Citgo sign and the Boston University Bridge.

above

MURALS OF THE BOSTON PUBLIC LIBRARY

STEPHANIE AHO
PENTAX K-1000

Eight stairway murals, by renowned French artist Pierre Puvis de Cha-vannes, adorn the walls of the McKim building's grand staircase and second floor gallery.

left

STATE HOUSE STAIRS

BEVERLY GRADY
FUJICA AX3, KODACHROME 64

After the railings on the main stair-case were cast, the molds were bro-ken to ensure they would remain one of a kind. The glass window's design is of a series of state seals Massachusetts has had since its settlement.

HALLOWED HALLS

BEVERLY GRADY
FUJICA AX3, KODACHROME 64

These halls of the State House are part of a large extension that was made to the original building between 1889-1895. The interior was made elegant with the extensive use of marble, wrought iron and carved wood paneling.

COURTYARD OF THE BOSTON PUBLIC LIBRARY

ANDREW P. DOUGLASS
MINOLTA, EPP

The Boston Public Library was founded in 1848 as the countries first large free municipal library. Copley Square has been its home since 1895 where it boasts 1.2 million rare books, manuscripts, maps, musical scripts and prints.

BOSTON PUBLIC LIBRARY

VIVIAN FRINK
CANON AE 1, KODAK KODACHROME

Resting in the sun in the courtyard of the Boston Public library.

VIEW FROM THE PRU

GORAN MATIJASEVIC
MINOLTA, FUJICHROME 100

From the Prudential Center, the
John Hancock Building reflects
the cityscape.

BOSTON MARATHON

COURTESY BOSTON ATHLETIC ASSOCIATION

The Boston Athletic Association was established in 1886 with the first Boston Marathon being held on April 19, 1897. Since then, the Boston Marathon has become the oldest annually running marathon.

GARGOYLE

RICHARD FERRARA
VIVITAR XV1, FUJI 100, F/4

This Trinity Church gargoyle looks
ready to take flight against the blue
of the John Hancock Tower.

BOSTON ARCHITECTURE

RICHARD FERRARA
MINOLTA X370N, KODAK EKTAR125, F/5.6

Boston's architecture is at its finest
all about Copley Square.

LOOKING UP

GORAN MATIJASEVIC
WIDELUX, KODACHROME 64

Downtown reflections sparkle in
the bright sun at Exchange Place in
the financial center.

REFLECTIONS

LAURA M. DEPAMPHILIS
MINOLTA SRT-SCII, FUJI SLIDE

The John Hancock Tower is a perfect mirror for the Trinity Church.

left

TRINITY CHURCH

BERNARD B. BARTICK
MINOLTA 3XI, SLIDE

Trinity Church, located on Copley Square is considered one of the most magnificent churches in this country.

opposite

JOHN HANCOCK AND TRINITY CHURCH

ANDREW P. DOUGLAS
BRONICA SQ PKR

The entrance to the observatory at the John Hancock offers a glassy image of the Trinity Church.

above

NIGHT LIGHTS

BEVERLY GRADY
CANON TL, KODAK 100

South Station glows from the city lights.

right

LIGHTS THE MOON

RODNEY R. HARRIS
CANON ELAN IIE, FUJI VELVIA, F/16

The John Hancock Tower is seen during the stillness of the morning.

opposite

THE JOHN HANCOCK FROM BELOW

HOWARD M. GOODMAN
CANON REBEL 2000, KODAK E100 VS, F/5.6

The John Hancock Tower with its sixty floors and 10,344 panes of glass provide a panoramic view of Boston.

HOT SUMMER DAY

RICHARD FERRARA
MINOLTA X370N, KODAK EKTAR125, F/5.6

Children cool off in the fountain of the
Christian Science building.

CITY DWELLING

GORAN MATIJASEVIC
MINOLTA, FUJICHROME 100

From the Prudential building, the
apartment buildings of Newbury
Street look like dollhouses.

IN THE SQUARE

GORAN MATIJASEVIC
WIDELUX, FUJICHROME 100

Across from the Boston Public Library
in Copley Square, one can enjoy reading
a book in the sun.

SPRINGTIME AT THE
CHRISTIAN SCIENCE BUILDING

LEN WICKENS
RICON, FUJI 100

Flowers are in full bloom near the reflecting pool. This is the world headquarters of the Church of Christ, Scientist.

RREADY, SET, GO!

ANDREW P. DOUGLASS
MINOLTA, EPP

The reflecting pool of the Christian Science building becomes an oasis for children in the summer.

left and opposite

MOTHER CHURCH

JUDITH E. SINGER
PENTAX 1QZOOM 928, KODAK 400

Mary Baker Eddy, founder of Christian Science, moved to Boston in 1881, two years after founding the Church. The Christian Science building was completed in 1895, with the dome extension completed in 1906.

left

NEWBURY STREET

ARLENE F. TALIADOROS
NIKON N90, FUJI 400

Sunday brunch on Newbury Street.

below

HARLEYS ON NEWBURY STREET

ARLENE F. TALIADOROS
NIKON N90, FUJI 400

Bikers enjoy an afternoon on Newbury Street. Do you think they were towed?

opposite

WINDOW SHOPPING

SAMUEL F. MICELI
CANON EOS REBEL, KODAK GOLD 200, F/5.6

An evening dress made of cocktail umbrellas attracts shoppers on Newbury Street.

CONTRIBUTORS

Richard Adams
115 Roberts Street
Quincy, MA 02169
rsa19@netzero.net
14, 16, 27, 32, 76, 99

Stephanie Aho
29 Brighton Street #2
Charlestown, MA 02129
saho55@hotmail.com
104

Babs Armour
411 West End Avenue #8E
New York, NY 10024
bka411@aol.com
back cover, 17, 18–19

Bernard B. Bartick
379 Wyassup Road
N. Stonington, CT 06359
BBesail@aol.com
114

Judith Austin Brown
61 Post 'N Rail Avenue
Plymouth, MA 02360
judyatthepond@aol.com
63, 100

Cynthia R. Cronig
47 Lakeside Drive East
Centerville, MA 02632
78

Stanley A. Cronig
47 Lakeside Drive East
Centerville, MA 02632
91

Robert A. Dennis
18 Orchard Crossing
Andover, MA 01810
rad1212@aol.com
43

Laura M. DePamphilis
38 Sterling Road
Hyannis, MA 02601
ldepam@aol.com
53, 114

Andrew P. Douglass
40 Chapel Street #3
Portsmouth, NH 03801
andy@northeastcolor.com
back cover, 36, 38–39, 66, 67,
71, 106, 115, 123

Joan R. Dunne
28 Sunning Road
Beverly, MA 01915
back cover, 45 (2), 52 (2)

Helen Eddy
26 Mt. Auburn Street
Cambridge, MA 02138
heleneddy@principia.edu
1, 3, 28, 30 (2), 54, 60, 72 (2)

Sara B. Edwards
15 Glenville Avenue Suite 6
Allston, MA 02134
ummmyup@hotmail.com
74

Richard Ferrara
9 Cushing Street
Amesbury, MA 01913
sightseen@worldnet.att.net
7, 29, 75, 110, 111, 118

William J. Ferrera
37 South Avenue
Melrose, MA 02176
12, 70

Vivian Frink
P.O. Box 3254
Bourne, MA 02532
dovimessages@aol.com
20, 21, 34, 51, 107

Howard M. Goodman
57 New Valley Road
New City, NY 10956
howgood@aol.com
31, 51, 116

David F. Gouveia
248 Winthrop Street
Taunton, MA 02780
36

Beverly Grady
34 Turkey Hill Road
West Newbury, MA 01985
58, 104, 105, 117

Rodney R. Harris
15 Vanderbilt Street
Randolph, MA 02368
rrhang@aol.com
40, 92, 117

Douglas Michael Houseman
109 Algonquin Road
Chestnut Hill, MA 02467
dhousman@jhmi.edu
98 (2), 99, 101

Ann L. Hurd
2855 Dartmouth Drive
Lancaster, CA 93536-5350
55, 56, 57

Sarah Lannon
P.O. Box 37
Greenbush, MA 02040
back cover, 10, 37, 44, 61

Michael Leonard
68 Ledgewood Drive
Yarmouth, ME 04096
mleonar1@maine.rr.com
26, 27, 33, 66, 77

Liz Ligon
41 Pearl Street
Medford, MA 02155
lizligon@hotmail.com
68

Goran Matijasevic
420 S. La Esperanza
San Clemente, CA 92672
goran_matijasevic@yahoo.com
8–9, 24 (2), 46 (2), 96, 101,
102–103, 108, 112–113, 119,
120–121

William Mattern
429 Country Way
Scituate, MA 02066
bgmatt@thecia.net
10, 60, 62, 80, 90

Samuel F. Miceli
15 Charles Street
Quincy, MA 02169
nomani151@cs.com
90, 127

Claudio Papapietro
24 Howard Street #2
Cambridge, MA 02139
cpapapietra@hotmail.com
5, 93

Jane Pedersen
5 Stowecraft Drive
Hampton, NH 03842
25, 41

Kevin and Susan Psaros
238 Charles St. #2
Malden, MA 02148
KevandsueP@aol.com
6, 22 (2), 23, 42, 69, 77, 78,
79, 81, 84, 85 (2), 94, 95

Peter Richman
22 Barberry Road
Lexington, MA 02421
prich33754@aol.com
49, 86, 87

Daniel Rudhardt
8 Plympton Street Apt. 42
Cambridge, MA 02138
rudhardt@deas.harvard.edu
58, 74

Barbara Ross
21, 81, 82, 81, 91, 97

Nelson Ross
59, 64–65

John D. Sidlo
32 Kilsyth Road #3
Brookline, MA 02445
jsidlo@world.std.com
89

Judith E. Singer
5 Fifer Lane
Lexington, MA 02420
124, 125

Arlene F. Taliadoros
35 John Wise Avenue
Essex, MA 01929
arlenef5@msn.com
11, 50, 96, 126 (2)

Marcella Wagner
91 Water Street
Stonington, CT 06378
Wagnermrcl@aol.com
13, 14, 48 (2)

Len Wickens
7 Flume Road
Magnolia, MA 01930
lwsw@prodigy.com
cover, 35, 47, 122

John D. Williams
140 Elm Street #5
Marblehead, MA 01945
johnrita@shore.net
73